Alphabet
B·O·O·K

AN ANGUS & ROBERTSON BOOK
An imprint of HarperCollinsPublishers

First published in Australia in 1991
This Bluegum edition published in 1992
CollinsAngus&Robertson Publishers Pty Limited (ACN 009 913 517)
A division of HarperCollinsPublishers (Australia) Pty Limited
25–31 Ryde Road, Pymble NSW 2073, Australia

HarperCollinsPublishers (New Zealand) Limited
31 View Road, Glenfield, Auckland 10, New Zealand

HarperCollinsPublishers Limited
77– 85 Fulham Palace Road, London W6 8JB, United Kingdom

National Library of Australia
Cataloguing-in-Publication data:

Gibbs, May, 1877–1969.
    Alphabet book.

    ISBN 0 207 16799 0.
    ISBN 0 207 17567 5 (paperback).

    1. Alphabet — Juvenile literature. 2. English language.
    Alphabet — Juvenile literature. I. Title.

421.1

Printed in Hong Kong

5 4 3 2 1
95 94 93 92

Alphabet
B·O·O·K

Angus&Robertson
An imprint of HarperCollins*Publishers*

A a

Adventuring

Babysitting

Bb

Cc

Cuddling

D d

Dressing up

Exploring

GOOD LUCK

Ee

F f

Fishing

Gossiping

Gg

Hh

Hiding

I'm important

Ii

J.j

Jingle-belling

Kissing

k

K

L1

Listening

Mm

Mother

Nestling

n

N

Oo

Oh!

Peeking

Pp

Queuing

Qq

Rr

Rescuing

Sharing

S s

T
t

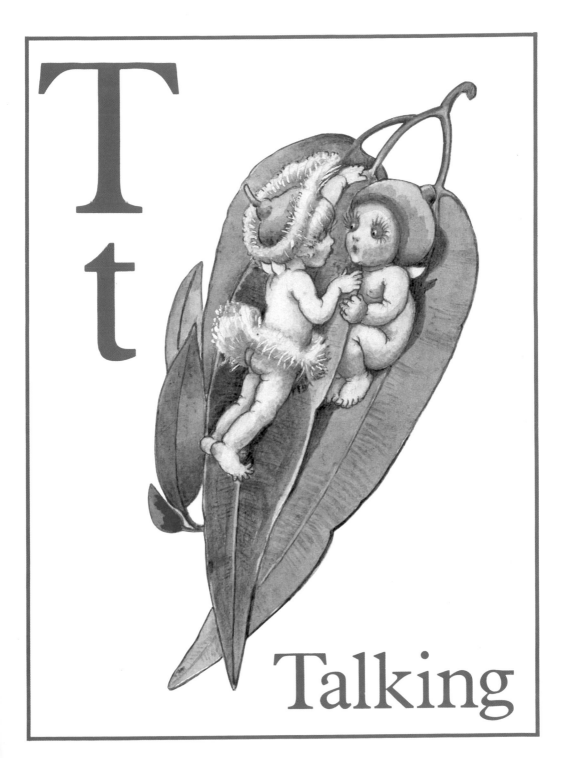

Talking

U u

Upside down

Visiting

Vv

Ww

Working

eXciting

X
X

Yy

Yawning

Zzzzzz

Zz

Aa	Adventuring
Bb	Babysitting
Cc	Cuddling
Dd	Dressing up
Ee	Exploring
Ff	Fishing
Gg	Gossiping
Hh	Hiding
Ii	I'm important
Jj	Jingle-belling
Kk	Kissing
Ll	Listening
Mm	Mother

Nn	Nestling
Oo	Oh!
Pp	Peeking
Qq	Queuing
Rr	Rescuing
Ss	Sharing
Tt	Talking
Uu	Upside down
Vv	Visiting
Ww	Working
Xx	eXciting
Yy	Yawning
Zz	Zzzzzz

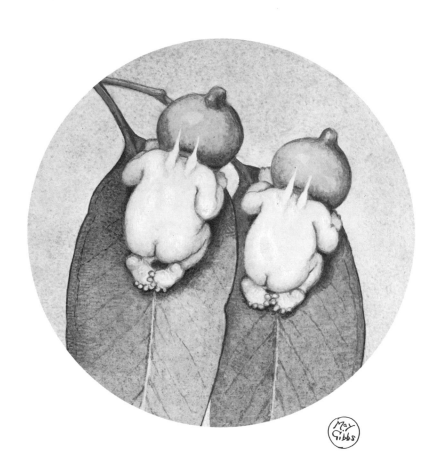